text by Valérie Mettais

Louvre

The Pocket Louvre

LOUVRE

MUSÉE DU
LOUVRE
ÉDITIONS

art
lys

Cover: **Leonardo da Vinci**,
Portrait of Lisa Gherardini del Giocondo,
known as "La Gioconda" or "Mona Lisa" (detail),
Florence, circa 1503-1506.
Oil on wood, 77 x 53 cm.
Opposite: Ieoh Ming Pei's glass pyramid
in the centre of the Napoleon courtyard, 1989
Page 4: the Louvre by night

CONTENTS

On 10 August 1793, barely a year after the 1st Republic was established, the Central Museum of Arts was opened at the *Palais du Louvre*, the former palace of the kings: a fitting heir to the Century of Enlightenment, this first public museum was housed in the *Salon carré* [Square drawing room], the *Grande Galerie* [Long Gallery] and the *Petite Galerie* [Small Gallery]. From the very outset, it boasted an impressive range of royal collections, which included works from the exhibition room of François I – *The Mona Lisa* was already there – and groups of paintings, drawings and sculptures assembled by Louis XIV as well as antiques held dear by Henry IV. This opulence was set to increase with the addition of the property of émigrés and the Church seized by the Revolution, followed by the spoils of war brought back by the *Directoire* [Executive Directory], and, soon afterwards, by the Empire. It was, in fact, in 1803 that the original Museum gave way to the *Musée Napoléon* [Napoleon Museum]; its rooms were designed by the architects Percier and Fontaine and they contained ever increasing numbers of works. In 1815, the fall of the Empire brought with it the end of the Louvre as it was then, with its collections being returned to defeated nations. With a few exceptions, however: for example, *The Marriage at Cana*, cumbersome and fragile, remained in Paris in an exchange deal.

Taking up the torch, the returning monarchy increased the number of acquisitions, made transfers and gave precedence to ancient civilisations: sculptures from the *Musée des Monuments Français* [Museum of French Monuments] went to the Louvre, followed by the twenty-four canvases by Rubens previously ordered by Marie de Medici for the *Palais de Luxembourg*; in 1821, Louis XVIII was given the *Venus de Milo*; in 1826, Champollion oversaw an "Egyptian Museum"; a year later the "Charles X Museum" was opened; in 1847 the "Assyrian museum" was set up. The 2nd Republic was not to be outdone: 1848 saw the opening of a Museum of Ethnography.

In the middle of the 19th century, the history of the museum reflected the political changes of its time. From 1852, Napoleon III entrusted the architects Visconti and Lefuel with the task of joining the Louvre to the Tuileries, creating new rooms and décors: major work was carried out during this period. May 1871 saw the Commune of Paris and the burning-down of the Tuileries palace. It was down to the 3rd Republic to add to the collections through donations and legacies, something which they did continuously, very soon leading to cramped conditions.

1981 saw the beginning of the Grand Louvre project, driven by François Mitterrand: the museum spread into the Richelieu wing, previously occupied by the Ministry of Finance; in the *cour Napoléon* [Napoleon Courtyard], the main entrance is now crowned by the glass pyramid created by Ieoh Ming Pei; the spaces have been re-designed, re-worked, restored, extended. And the work is still going on. With its eight departments and three hundred thousand works, thirty-five thousand of which are displayed over an area covering sixty thousand square metres, the Louvre is one of the biggest and richest museums in the world today. The seven million or so visitors who pass through its doors each year can vouch for it.

Foundations of the fortress and towers built by Philip Augustus at the end of the 12th century.

Because he wanted to protect his capital, the king ordered the construction of an enclosure uniting the two banks of the Seine. To the west of Paris, at the place known as Lupara, the fortress consisted of ten towers with, at its centre, a keep fifteen metres in diameter and more than thirty metres high, with a draw-bridge and a dry moat and housing a few residences. From "Lupara" to "Louvre", this keep, this "Great Tower", derived its name. Two centuries later, the city grew and acquired a new enclosure; Charles V made it his place of residence – spacious, embellished and with an open outlook. Other kings carried on his work, transforming the Louvre into a vast royal palace.

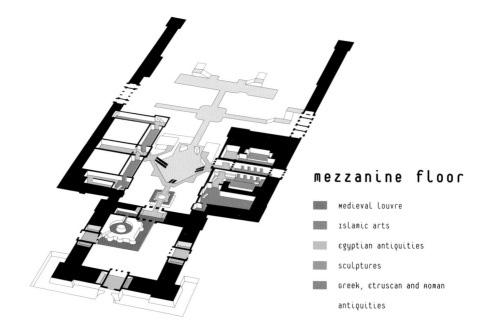

mezzanine floor

- medieval louvre
- islamic arts
- egyptian antiquities
- sculptures
- greek, etruscan and roman antiquities

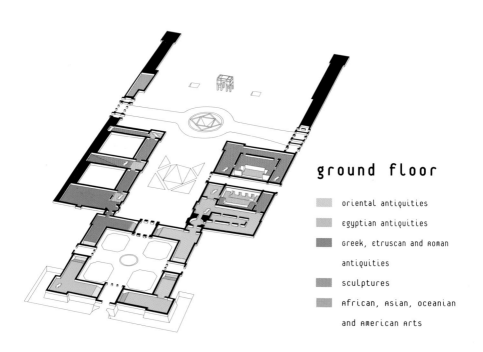

ground floor

- oriental antiquities
- egyptian antiquities
- greek, etruscan and roman antiquities
- sculptures
- african, asian, oceanian and american arts

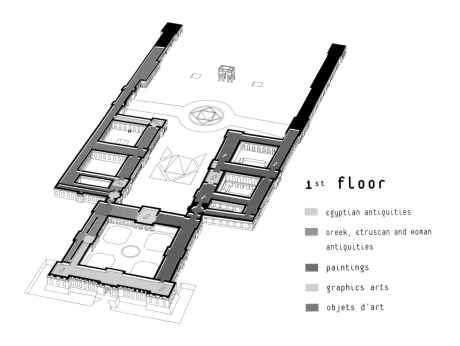

1st floor

egyptian antiquities

greek, etruscan and roman antiquities

paintings

graphics arts

objets d'art

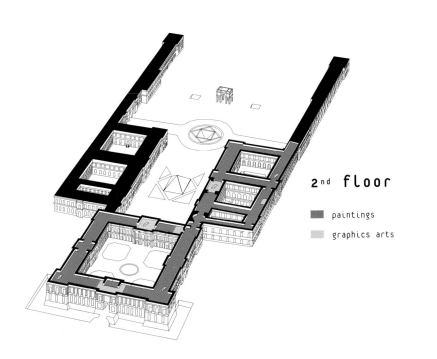

2nd floor

paintings

graphics arts

This work is located in the **Richelieu wing**, on the **ground floor**

ORIENTAL ANTIQUITIES

Winged bulls with human heads.
Khorsabad (Iraq),
courtyard of the palace of Sargon II
of Assyria, 713-706 BC.
Gypseous alabaster, h: 440 cm.

WHAT IS THIS WRITING?

It is more than three centuries since some strange signs engraved in stone, bricks and metal were discovered in Mesopotamia. Made up of marks resembling nail heads, the "cuneiform" characters were originally etched, using a reed, in tablets of soft clay; these earliest written testimonies date from the end of the 4th millennium BC. First used in the Sumerian language, they could be found everywhere: on the back of a dignitary's statue, on a stele depicting a king's victory, on a relief celebrating the foundation of a temple.

These works are located in the **Richelieu wing**, on the **ground floor**

Statue of the official Ebih-il.
Mari (Syria), Temple of Ishtar, circa 2400 BC.
Alabaster, eyes lined with bitumen and incrusted with shell and lapis-lazuli, h: 52.5 cm.

Stele of Vultures ("historic" side).
Tello (ancient Girsu, State of Lagash, Iraq), circa 2450 BC.
Limestone, h: 180 cm.

Ur-Nanshe relief, Prince of Lagash.
Tello (ancient Girsu,
State of Lagash, Iraq),
circa 2500 BC.
Limestone, h: 40 cm.

Power, wisdom and equity: sovereigns owe all this to the gods. Whilst Gudea, or "The Chosen One", ruled the Lagash dynasty, in Southern Mesopotamia, further to the North and four centuries later, Hammurabi founded the first kingdom of Babylon; by the ring and sceptre, the god Shamash gave him his authority. With almost three hundred paragraphs, a Code of laws existed to ensure justice was served: if someone put out someone else's eye, that person had their own eye put out; if a doctor botched an operation his wrist was cut off; if a woman dishonoured her husband, she was thrown into the water to drown.

These works are located in the **Richelieu wing,** on the **ground floor**

Gudea, Prince of Lagash, with the gushing vase. Tello (ancient Girsu, State of Lagash, Iraq), circa 2150 BC. Diorite, h: 62 cm.

The Code of Hammurabi,
sovereign of Babylon (detail).
Stele carried off as war booty to
Susa (Iran),
circa 1792-1750 BC.
Basalt, h: 225 cm.

It was in the city of Susa, in Elam, in this "high country", that Darius the Great founded the political capital of the Persian Achaemenid empire, which continuously annexed immense territories, from the Greek Islands to the banks of the Indus River. And because he wanted to bring countries and people together within one universal empire, the king incorporated a wide range of styles into his palace: an Iranian-style Great Hall of Audience, a décor of enamelled bricks inspired by Babylon, bull-head capitals, worthy heirs of Assyrian colossi, scrolls from Ionia and Egyptian-inspired motifs.

⟨ *Winged bulls with human heads*, pp. 10-11.

Bushel decorated with hunters, dogs and ibexes.
Susa (Iran), necropolis,
circa 4200-3500 BC.
Painted terracotta, h: 28.9 cm.

Elamite praying figure.
Susa (Iran), acropolis,
12th century BC.
Gold and bronze, h: 7.5 cm.

_ Top
Grand bull-head capital.
Susa (Iran), audience room *(apadana)*
of the palace of Darius the Great,
King of Persia, circa 520-500 BC.
Limestone, h: 552 cm.

_ Above
Frieze of Archers.
Susa (Iran), palace of Darius the Great,
King of Persia,
circa 500 BC.
Enamelled bricks, h: 200 cm.

Human depiction, in its various forms, from the highly recognisable to the not so recognisable, often represents an enigma for archaeologists. At Safadi, a workshop churned out ivory statuettes which were all very similar: what was their intended purpose? Were they mere mortals? In Northern Syria, a terra- cotta object appears to be an "idol", an image of an adored deity as if it was the deity itself. At Ugarit, two thousand years later, El, god of the Heavens, Anat, Goddess of War and Fertility, and Baal, the Storm god were all worshipped and depictions of them placed in temples.

These works are located in the **Sully area**, on the **ground floor**

_ Top, left
Male statuette.
Safadi (The Negev region, Israel),
3500-3000 BC.
Hippopotamus tooth, h: 24 cm.

_ Below, left
Stele of Baal with a thunderbolt.
Ugarit (Syria),
14th-13th Century BC.
Limestone, h: 142 cm.

_ Opposite
Idol with eyes.
Northern Syria,
circa 3300-3000 BC.
Terracotta, h: 27 cm.

Hunt patera.
Ugarit (Syria), Temple of Baal,
14th-12th century BC.
Gold, diameter: 18.8 cm.

ISLAMIC ARTS

Peacock dish (detail).
Iznik (Turkey), 1540-1555.
Siliceous ceramic with decoration
painted on slip and under
transparent glaze,
diameter: 37.5 cm.

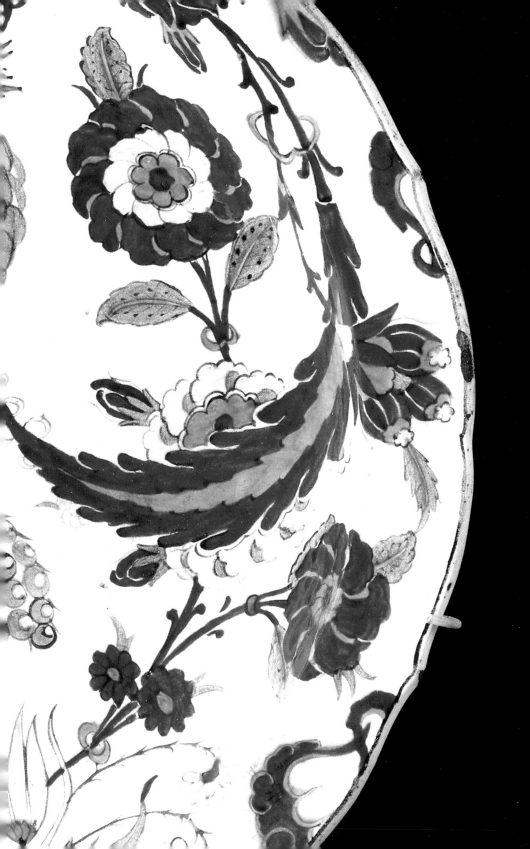

Islam, "surrender to God", was preached in the 7th century by the Prophet Mohammed, the "Highly Praised One". Allah is the one, the only, creator and judge, and his word is the Koran, the "Ultimate reading". Muslims, the "Believers", obey its commandments. In 622 began the Hegira, the "Flight" of the Prophet from Mecca to Medina: the Muslim era began here. From this point, the Islam civilisation flourished, bringing together people from a diversity of cultures, from Spain to India. The Arabs, "desert dwellers", nomads from the Arabian peninsula, turn their language into the expression of the new religion.

These works are located in the **Richelieu wing,** on the **mezzanine floor**

Celestial sphere,
by the astrolabe maker
Yunus ibn al-Husayn. Baghdad (?)
[Iraq] or Ispahan (Iran), 1145.
Cast copper alloy, engraved and
inlaid with silver, diameter: 16.5 cm.

Pyxis in the name of al-Mughira,
son of the caliph 'Abd al-Rahman III.
Madinat al-Zahra (Spain), 968.
Sculpted and engraved ivory,
h: 15 cm.

Panel with a stylised bird,
tympanum fragment.
Egypt, late 9th-early 10th century.
Aleppo pine, h: 73 cm.

IS THERE ANY UNITY?

Sometimes moving from country to country according to the will of princes, reflecting the same faith and always drawing on local traditions, the craftsmen of Islam marked their creations with stylistic rules: divided into registers, repeated and often symmetrical, geometric décors cover walls and objects; forms are streamlined, hence dynamic and expressive; the calligraphy delivers its messages while following natural curves; wild or domestic animals, realistic or stylised, are familiar motifs.

The Kufic inscription reminds us that:
"Science, its taste is bitter at the beginning but, at the end, sweeter than honey."

These works are located in the **Richelieu wing**, on the **mezzanine floor**

Large dish with epigraphic decoration, known as the *"Science dish".*
Khorasan or Transoxiana (Iran), 10th-11th century. Clay ceramic with slip decoration under transparent glaze, diameter: 38.8 cm.

Lion perfume burner.
Khorasan (Iran), 11th-12th century.
Cast bronze with openwork decoration, engraved and incrusted with glass paste (?), 28.2 x 32 cm.

Bowl with falconer horseman.
Iran, early 13th century.
Siliceous ceramic with a lustred
decoration embellished with gold
on opacified glaze,
diameter: 22 cm

These works are located in the **Richelieu wing**, on the **mezzanine floor**

Bowl, known as the "Baptistery of St Louis", made by **Muhammad ibn al-Zayn**. Syria or Egypt, early 14th century. Hammered brass, chased and inlaid with gold, silver and black paste, h: 23 cm.

_ Top

The Archangel Gabriel reveals Sura VIII (The Spoils) to the Prophet, page from the *Siyar-e Nabi (Life of the Prophet)*. Istanbul, 1594-1595. Pigments and gold on paper, 37.5 x 27.3 cm.

_ Above, left

Mosque lamp in the name of Sultan Nasir al-Din Hasan. Egypt or Syria, 1347-1361. Blown glass decorated with enamel and gilt, h: 35.5 cm.

Vase in the name of Sultan al-Malik al-Nasir Salah al-Din Yusuf, known as the "*Barberini Vase*". Damascus or Aleppo (Syria), 1237-1260. Hammered brass with repoussé decoration engraved and inlaid with re-engraved silver, h: 45 cm.

EGYPTIAN ANTIQUITIES

Harvest and preparation of the earth,
painting from the tomb of Ounsou.
Left bank of Thebes (Luxor),
New Kingdom, 18th dynasty,
circa 1450 BC.
Paint on silt, 94 x 68 cm.

IS THERE A BEGINNING TO CIVILISATION?

Placed under the protection of the falcon Horus, the "Distant One", who transfers his powers to a Pharaoh, the 1st dynasty of the Egyptian monarchy began with the political unification of the kingdoms of the north and south of the country, the development of the Nile Valley and the creation of a writing system: hieroglyphics. Auspicious beginnings for a civilisation which was to prove itself blessed with stability and longevity, constructing its temples and tombs throughout thirty dynasties, representing more than three thousand years.

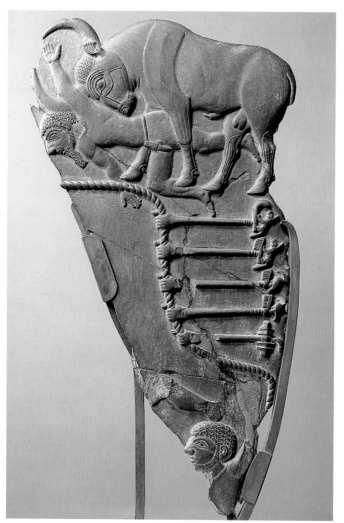

These works are located in the **Sully area,** on the **1st floor**

Bull palette.
Nagada civilisation,
circa 3150 BC.
Schist, h: 26.5 cm.

Dagger. Gebel el-Arak (?),
in Southern Abydos,
Nagada civilisation, circa 3300-3200 BC.
Flint blade, shaft made from
the canine tooth of a hippopotamus,
h: 25.5 cm.

Stele of the Snake King or the Horus Djet.
Abydos, royal necropolis,
1st dynasty,
circa 3100 BC.
Limestone, h: 143 cm.

WHY ARE THEY IN PROFILE AND FULL-FACE, OR ENTIRELY FRONT-ON?

Because there is a sense of magic about it, because to depict a man or an animal amounts to breathing life into him or it, representation in Egypt complies with immutable codes, respecting ancient traditions, in keeping with the world order established by the gods. In paintings and reliefs, the body is in profile, except for the torso; the eye is full-face; objects are positioned vertically. The goal is to present everything with the utmost clarity, since everything must be recognisable. Frontality reigns in sculptures; sometimes private statuary bends the rules: the scribe's head is just slightly raised.

These works are located in the **Sully area**, on the **1ˢᵗ floor**

_ Top
Head of King Didoufri.
Abou Roach, temple,
Old Kingdom, 4ᵗʰ dynasty,
circa 2560 BC.
Red sandstone, h: 26 cm.

_ Above
Stele of Nefertiabet.
Giza, the princess's tomb,
Old Kingdom, 4ᵗʰ dynasty,
circa 2590 BC. Painted limestone,
37.5 x 52.5 cm.

Squatting scribe.
Saqqara, Old Kingdom,
4th or 5th dynasty, circa 2620-2350 BC.
Painted limestone, eyes inlaid
with rock crystal and alabaster
and ringed with copper, h: 53.7 cm.

He was the embodiment of the gods on earth, he was simultaneously priest, warrior, governor and administrator: the pharaoh held absolute powers. "Pharaoh", means "great house" in Egyptian, he who represents and occupies the royal palace. With a false beard or several crowns, he took on all sorts of appearances. As a sphinx with the body of a lion, placed along avenues leading to temples or necropolises, he protected sacred places from enemy forces. On his death, statues, furniture and funereal texts accompanied him on his journey to the beyond.

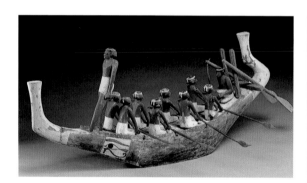

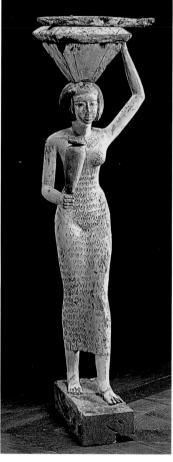

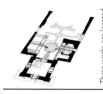

These works are located in the **Sully area**, on the **mezzanine floor** on the **ground floor**

_ Top

Model of a boat, navigation scene.
Assiout, tomb of Chancellor Nakhti,
Middle Kingdom,
12th dynasty, circa 1900 BC.
Painted wood, 38.5 x 81 cm.

_ Left

Hippopotamus.
Early Middle Kingdom,
circa 2000-1900 BC.
Egyptian "faience" (compressed quartz
granules covered with a glaze), h: 12.7 cm.

_Opposite
Offering bearer.
Assiout, early Middle Kingdom,
circa 1950 BC.
Stuccoed and painted ficus wood,
h: 108 cm.

Great sphinx.
Tanis, Middle Kingdom,
12th dynasty,
circa 1850 BC.
Pink granite, h: 183 cm.

From the beginning of his reign, Amenhotep, the fourth to bear the name, undermined the very foundations of royalty, established by tradition: religion, places of worship, the seat of power, even the canons of representation. The Sun Disk, Aten, was worshipped as the sole god; at Karnak, temples were open-air; an entirely new capital was established, Akhet-Aten, the "Horizon of the Disk"; the pharaoh, his wife Nefertiti and their six daughters are shown with elongated bodies, sometimes deformed, often realistic and sensual. After his reign, everything relating to this Akhenaten was erased or destroyed.

These works are located in the **Sully area,** on the **1st floor**

Statue of Queen Nefertiti (?).
El-Amarna (?),
New Kingdom, 18th dynasty,
circa 1353-1337 BC. Crystallised red sandstone, h: 29 cm.

Statuette of Akhenaten and Nefertiti.
El-Amarna,
New Kingdom, 18th dynasty,
circa 1353-1337 BC.
painted limestone, h: 22.5 cm.

Colossal statue of King Amenhotep IV,
or Akhenaten.
East Karnak, New Kingdom,
18th dynasty,
circa 1353-1337 BC.
Painted sandstone, h: 137 cm.

HOW ARE THE DEAD ACCOMPANIED?

"Homage to thee, O my divine father Osiris! I shall possess my flesh for ever, I shall not become corruption, I shall not decay, I shall not turn into worms; I exist, I live, I am strong, I have awakened in peace, my intestines shall not perish [...], my flesh is permanent, it shall not perish, it shall never be destroyed in this land", is written in the Book of the Dead. To help the deceased rise from the dead and protect his remains, such was the purpose of mummification which, in the Egypt of the Pharaohs, took a period of seventy days. It was still practised during the Roman and Coptic periods.

These works are located in the **Sully area**, on the **ground floor**

Funerary stele of Taperet.
Third Intermediate Period,
22nd dynasty, circa 900-800 BC.
Stuccoed and painted wood,
31 x 29 cm.

Sarcophagus of Chancellor Imeneminet
(coffin and lid),
Third Intermediate Period,
25th-26th dynasty,
circa 700-600 BC.
Stuccoed and painted wood, h: 188 cm.

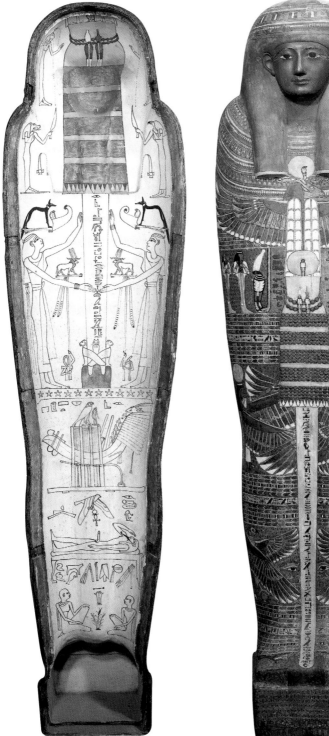

Christ and Abbot Mena.
Baouit Monastery,
Coptic art, 7th century.
Tempera on sycamore fig wood,
57 x 57 cm.

Funerary portrait of a young woman,
known as a *"Portrait of Fayoum".*
Antinoe, Romano-Egyptian art,
2nd century.
Wax painting on cedar wood,
42 x 24 cm.

GREEK, ETRUSCAN AND ROMAN ANTIQUITIES

Athena and Hermes watching a battle,
detail of a red-figured amphora
made by the potter **Andokides**.
Attic workshop, circa 530 BC.
Terracotta, h: 58 cm.

DOES A CRAFTSMAN HAVE FREEDOM OF A CITY?

Without architects to construct sanctuaries, without sculptors to place statues of deities and heroes inside them, without painters or potters to produce vases destined for tombs, without foundry workers to produce coins, the Greek city could not survive.

However, it attached little importance to a craftsman: whilst he was a demiourgos, a "demiurge" or "public worker" who, for the good of everyone, received knowledge and experience from the gods, he was also a banausos, a labourer responsible for manual, vulgar and unworthy tasks. By signing their work, craftsmen gradually claimed more social respect.

These works are located in the **Denon wing**, on the **mezzanine floor**

_ Top

Fragment of a female statuette.
Cyclades Islands, Early Bronze Age
(or Early Cycladic Age),
circa 2700-2400 BC.
Marble, h: 18.5 cm.

_ Left

Head of a horseman, known as the
"Rampin Horseman". Athens acropolis,
Archaic Period, circa 550-540 BC.
Marble with traces of polychromy,
h: 27 cm.

_ Opposite
Statue of a woman, know as the
"Woman of Auxerre".
Crete (?), Archaic Period,
Daedalic style, circa 630 BC.
Limestone, h: 75 cm.

Red-figured calyx-crater,
Hercules versus the giant Antaeus,
made by the painter **Euphronios**.
Attic workshop, Archaic Period,
circa 510 BC.
Terracotta, h: 45 cm.

WHO INVENTED STATUES?

Entering a temple, Hercules came face to face with a figure that was none other than his own representation: feeling threatened, he raised his weapon. The author of this effigy was an Athenian hero, simultaneously a sculptor, architect, blacksmith, engineer and inventor of tools – the hatchet, the drill, the plumb line... His name was Daedalus and he excelled at making statues of gods who started moving by themselves and whose eyes, it is said, he opened, statues that were so lifelike that they had to be chained up at night to stop them from escaping. So went one of Greek sculpture's great myths.

These works are located in the **Sully area,** on the **ground floor**

Procession of the Panathenaea (detail), plaque from the frieze of the Parthenon, Athens acropolis, Classical Period, 438-431 BC. Marble, 96 x 207 cm.

Aphrodite, known as the *Venus of Arles*.
Roman copy of a statue attributed
to **Praxiteles** (Athens, Classical
Period, 4th century BC).
Marble, h: 194 cm.

Combatant warrior,
known as the *"Borghese Gladiator"*,
statue produced by **Agasias of Ephesus**.
Antium, Hellenistic Period,
circa 100 BC.
Marble, h: 157 cm.

These works are located in the **Denon wing**, on the **1st floor**

"*Venus de Milo*".
Melos,
Hellenistic Period,
circa 100 BC.
Marble, h: 202 cm.

Winged Victory of Samothrace.
Samothrace,
Hellenistic Period,
circa 190 BC.
Marble, h: 328 cm.

The Etruscan civilisation made a name for itself on several fronts: for its language and writing, for its religious practices, for its art of reading the future in the livers of sacrificed animals, for the elevated social standing of its women, for its wine trade, for its paint-ed terracotta ware, its bronze-work and silverware. Not forgetting its princely tombs and murals, exact copies of the homes of the living, complete with entranceways leading to several rooms and wall decorations. Known to the Romans as "Tusci", the Etruscans gave their name to the region of Tuscany.

These works are located in the **Denon wing**, on the **ground floor**

"*Sarcophagus of the spouses*",
a double cinerary urn.
Tomb of Cerveteri
(Central Italy),
circa 510 BC.
Painted terracotta, h: 114 cm.

Wall plaque,
known as the *"Campana plaque"* (detail).
Tomb of Cerveteri (Central Italy),
circa 530-520 BC.
Painted terracotta, h: 118 cm.

◆➤ DOES ROME HAVE A LEGEND?

To link it history to that of the Greeks, the Roman Empire sought an identity for itself in a distant ancestor: Aeneas, the Trojan hero. To endow itself with a divine principle, it introduced Mars, the War God, who visited a woman and gave her twins, Romulus and Remus. But the twins were thrown into the Tiber, washed up on a riverbank and fed by a she-wolf before being brought up by a shepherd. Appointed king by an omen, Romulus marked out a furrow with his plough representing the outer limit of the future city of Rome. Jealous, Remus crossed this sacred line, and his brother killed him. This foundation dates back to 753 BC.

❮ Poussin, p. 65.

❮ David, p. 74.

These works are located in the **Denon wing**, on the **ground floor**

_ Top
Sarcophagus: "The lion hunt".
Rome, circa 235-240.
Marble, 88 x 220 cm.

_ Left
Goblet with skeletons.
Boscoreale treasure, near Pompeii,
1st century.
Gilded silver, h: 10.4 cm.

_Opposite
Portrait of the Emperor Hadrian.
Rome, second quarter
of the 2nd century.
Bronze, h: 43 cm.

The Phoenix.
Antioch (Turkey),
courtyard of a villa, 6th century.
Marble and limestone
pavement mosaic, 600 x 425 cm.

PAINTINGS

Paolo Caliari, known as **Veronese**,
The Wedding Feast at Cana (detail),
Venice, 1562-1563.
Oil on canvas, 677 x 994 cm.

WHAT IS A PORTRAIT?

In depicting the outline of the shadow of a cherished face on a wall, a young girl found herself the inventor of painting. The emergence of portraits fits in well with this ancient legend – in most languages, the word "portrait" comes from "portray" meaning to depict in a drawing or painting. In the 14th and 15th centuries increasing numbers of effigies of sovereigns with distinctive features appeared, doubtless bearing a likeness, often idealised. In imitation of medals, the profile stands out against a background of gold, a décor or a landscape before being replaced by face-on or three-quarter portraits.

‹ Italian portraits of the 15th century, pp. 88-89.

These works are located in the **Richelieu wing**, on the **2nd floor**

Painter working in Paris,
Portrait of John the Good, King of France,
circa 1350.
Tempera on wood, 60 x 44 cm.

Jean Fouquet,
Portrait of Charles VII, King of France,
Tours, circa 1445-1450.
Tempera on wood, 85.7 x 70.6 cm.

To touch those looking at it, to have them feel pity in the face of the pain and death of Christ, such were the aims of pictures of Christian worship. A Pietà depicts the Virgin Mary carrying or supporting on her knees the body of her son, following the Descent from the cross; at the end of the Middle Ages this was referred to as a "Virgin of Pity" painting. The divine is there, witnessing the scene – God the Father, angels and the dove of the Holy Spirit. Those on earth honour, pray and weep – John the Apostle and Evangelist, Mary Magdalene and a canon as the donor.

These works are located in the **Richelieu wing**, on the **2nd floor**

Jean Malouel,
Pietà, known as the *Large Round Pietà*,
Dijon, circa 1400.
Tempera on wood, diameter: 64.5 cm.

Inscription in Latin engraved on a gold background:
"Come all you who pass my way, look and see whether
there is any suffering like my suffering"
(first Lamentation of Jeremiah).

Enguerrand Quarton,
Pietà of Villeneuve-lès-Avignon,
Avignon, circa 1455.
Tempera on wood, 163 x 218 cm.

HOW CAN THE KING'S BELOVED BE PORTRAYED?

At Fontainebleau, where Francis I had his palace built in the new Renaissance style, a new type of court art emerged: using eroticism under the guise of mythology, manipulating poetic allusion, it glorified the body of women and magnified the presence of sovereigns. Here was an art of royal essence. Half a century later, Henry IV followed suit; solemn and informal, naked in a bath, the portrait of his mistress Gabrielle d'Estrées is a loving allegory, the stiff nipple and the held-out ring symbolising a forthcoming pregnancy and marriage.

These works are located in the **Richelieu wing,** on the **2nd floor**

Fontainebleau school,
Diana the Huntress,
circa 1550.
Oil on canvas, 191 x 132 cm.

Jean Clouet (attributed to),
Portrait of François I, King of France,
Paris, circa 1530.
Oil on wood, 96 x 74 cm.

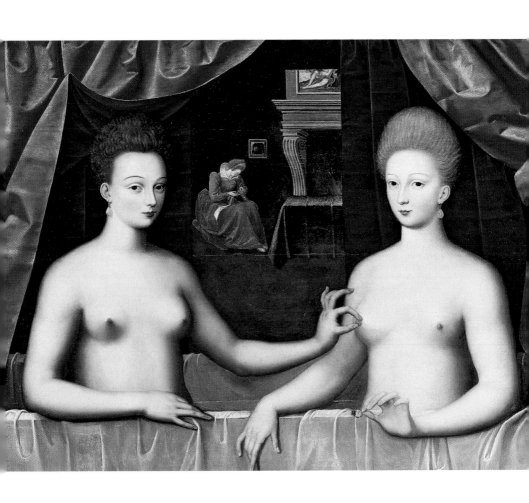

Fontainebleau school,
Gabrielle d'Estrées
and one of her sisters in the bath,
circa 1595.
Oil on wood, 96 x 125 cm.

WHAT IS LA TOUR REVEALING TO US, WHAT IS LE NAIN HIDING FROM US?

A parable is a story that has an underlying moral or religious lesson, sometimes without being obvious. When time has passed and their culture is different, the audience may have trouble deciphering what the artist has put in his work. With figures depicted in the light and in the dark, La Tour contemplates innocence, temptation and deception, the vanity of human things and the quest for truth in the shadows. In more colourful surroundings, the Le Nain brothers are perhaps looking for similar things.

These works are located in the **Sully area,** on the **2nd floor**

Louis or **Antoine Le Nain**,
Family of peasants indoors,
Paris, circa 1640-1645.
Oil on canvas, 113 x 159 cm.

_ Top
Georges de La Tour,
The repenting Magdalene,
Lunéville, circa 1640-1645.
Oil on canvas, 128 x 94 cm.

_ Above
Georges de La Tour,
The Cheat with the ace of diamonds,
Lunéville, circa 1635.
Oil on canvas, 107 x 146 cm.

Recently founded and composed mainly of soldiers, Rome needed wives to form a people. Romulus set a trap for the Sabines, his neighbours: at his signal, during a celebration, every Roman soldier threw himself on a Sabine woman and took her away. Everything then exploded, as Poussin shows. A century and a half later, David would depict the end of the story, when the Sabine men came to reclaim their women, who in the meantime had become mothers of little Romans. It was the Sabine women who were to ask for peace.

⟨ David, p. 74.

These works are located in the **Richelieu wing**, on the **2nd floor**

Nicolas Poussin,
Self-Portrait,
Rome, 1650.
Oil on canvas, 98 x 74 cm.

Nicolas Poussin,
The rape of the Sabine women,
Rome, circa 1637-1638.
Oil on canvas, 159 x 206 cm.

HOW DO YOU CHOOSE THE RIGHT MOMENT?

In 41 BC, Cleopatra VII, Queen of Egypt, met the Roman chief Anthony at Tarsus, in Asia Minor; she married him and, with him, attempted to create an Eastern empire. Claude Lorrain depicts this historic and passionate meeting, giving it a glowing red setting. In 1662, Catherine de Champaigne, a nun at the Port-Royal Jansenist abbey, recovered from paralysis of the legs. To give thanks for the grace of God, her father brought the moment of Mother Superior's prayer and the time of the miracle together in a painting.

These works are located in the **Sully area,** on the 2nd floor

_ Above, detail of the painting on the righthand page
Claude Gellée, known as **le Lorrain**,
The Disembarkation of Cleopatra at Tarsus,
Rome, 1642-1643.
Oil on canvas, 119 x 170 cm.

_ Opposite
Philippe de Champaigne,
Ex-voto of 1662,
Paris, 1662.
Oil on canvas, 165 x 229 cm.

The painter wrote in Latin: "Christ, the only physician of body and soul. Sister Catherine Suzanne de Champaigne, after a fever lasting fourteen months that had frightened doctors with its tenacity and the intensity of its symptoms, when almost half of her body was paralysed, when nature was already exhausted and the doctors had abandoned her, having joined Mother Catherine Agnès in prayer and recovering perfect health in an instant, offers herself again. Philippe de Champaigne presented this image of such a great miracle as testimony to his joy in 1662".

There is the ceremonial portrait, with drapes, horse and footmen, which indicates a high dignitary, and there is the overpowering, majestic portrait, in which the absolute monarch brandishes the signs of his power: the ceremonial wig, the immense coronation cloak decorated with golden lilies on a blue background and lined with ermine, the sword, sceptre and crown, shoes with red heels, the column base and the red velvet embroidered with gold are the signs of nobility and royalty – the "fleur de lis" also referred to the brand applied to the shoulders of convicts.

These works are located in the **Sully area**, on the **2nd floor**

Charles Le Brun,
Chancellor Séguier,
Paris, circa 1655-1657.
Oil on canvas, 295 x 351 cm.

Hyacinthe Rigaud,
Louis XIV, King of France,
Versailles, 1701.
Oil on canvas, 277 x 194 cm.

WHAT IS A GENRE?

To be admitted to the Royal Academy, a painter had to present a reception piece. If he worked in a major genre – biblical, ancient and mythological history –, he would be better paid and would be provided with a place to live and a pension. If he chose smaller genres – portrait, landscape, genre scenes and still life –, he had a more uncertain future. But there was a crack in the hierarchy: in 1717, with a pilgrimage, Watteau was accredited as a painter of "fêtes galantes", a genre he created; in 1728, with a ray, Chardin was admitted as a "painter of flowers, fruits and genre subjects", accumulating genres and praise.

These works are located in the **Sully area**, on the **2nd floor**

Jean-Baptiste Siméon Chardin,
The Ray,
Paris, 1728.
Oil on canvas, 114 x 146 cm.

DO PAINTERS SLIP SECRETS INTO THEIR PAINTINGS?

Often, it is the details in a painting that clarify a scene: The Goddess Diana returns from hunting; on the ground lie arrows and game. Sometimes, the very intimacy of these details means that they are shown more discreetly. At her engagement, a young woman lifts the hem of her apron to reveal something; at her feet, a hen looks after her brood. In a bedroom, to the left of a couple, a bed is unmade, the sheets crumpled, an apple discarded and a vase knocked over. In order to paint what they cannot show – union, seduction and desire –, Greuze and Fragonard leave little clues that have to be solved.

These works are located in the **Sully area**, on the **2nd floor**

François Boucher,
Diana leaving her bath,
Paris, 1742.
Oil on canvas, 56 x 73 cm.

Jean-Baptiste Greuze,
The Village Bride,
Paris, 1761.
Oil on canvas, 92 x 117 cm.

Jean Honoré Fragonard,
The Bolt,
Paris, circa 1778.
Oil on canvas, 73 x 93 cm.

When a former general-in-chief of a revolutionary army becomes emperor, he needs to make the regime change legitimate. Napoleon I thus asked his official painter to depict his coronation, or rather to arrange its depiction. The moment chosen is when, already crowned by himself, he crowns his wife. Carefully assembled and detai-led, everyone is there, family, ministers, nobility and clergy. Everyone, even those who were absent: in the gallery, Letizia Bonaparte, or Madame Mère ["Madam Mother"], was added; and the foreground, left empty, opens onto another absentee from the scene: the painting's viewer.

‹ Poussin, p. 65.

These works are located in the **Denon wing,** on the 1ˢᵗ **floor**

Jacques Louis David,
The Intervention of the Sabine Women,
Paris, 1799.
Oil on canvas, 385 x 522 cm.

Jacques Louis David,
Coronation of Napoleon I in Notre-Dame,
2 December 1804,
Paris, 1806-1807.
Oil on canvas, 621 x 979 cm.

"To call oneself romantic and look systematically to the past is a contradiction"; and Charles Baudelaire continues: "Romanticism and modern art are one and the same thing". Whilst Géricault depicted in large format the survivors of a shipwreck that was widely talked about under the Restoration, Delacroix also used large format to exalt the barricades erected by a revolution to overcome a king – on 25 July 1830, the Prefect of Paris had, nevertheless, offered reassurances to Charles X: "Whatever you do, Paris won't move". A romantic paints death, today's history, sensuality and the elsewhere.

These works are located in the **Denon wing,** on the **1ˢᵗ floor**

Théodore Géricault,
Portrait of Woman with Gambling Mania,
Paris, 1822.
Oil on canvas, 77 x 64 cm.

Théodore Géricault,
The Raft of the Medusa,
Paris, 1819.
Oil on canvas, 491 x 716 cm.

Eugène Delacroix,
The Death of Sardanapalus,
Paris, 1827.
Oil on canvas, 392 x 496 cm.

_ Top

Eugène Delacroix,
The 28th of July 1830:
Liberty guiding the people,
Paris, 1830.
Oil on canvas, 260 x 325 cm.

_ Above

Eugène Delacroix,
Women of Algiers in their apartment,
Paris, 1834.
Oil on canvas, 180 x 229 cm.

A Professor at the School of Fine Arts, Ingres taught the primacy of line and respect for the old canon; "drawing is everything, it is art itself", he wrote. "The material processes of painting are very easy and can be learned in eight days." However, he took remarkable liberties with line as well as with the bodies of women, combining, exaggerating and distorting, elongating a back, moving a breast. He did this to increase the strength of expression and the delight of the look. Khalil Bey, owner of *The Turkish Bath*, was also the owner of Courbet's *The Origin of the World* (Musée d'Orsay).

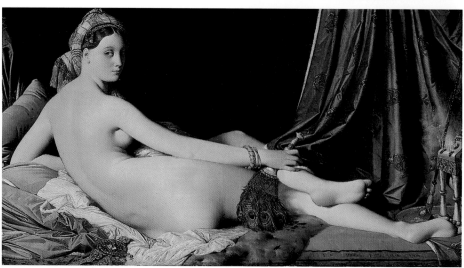

These works are located in the **Denon wing**, on the **1st floor**

_ Top

Hippolyte Flandrin,
Nude youth sitting by the sea, Study,
Rome, 1836.
Oil on canvas, 98 x 124 cm.

_ Above

Jean Auguste Dominique Ingres,
La Grande Odalisque,
Rome, 1814.
Oil on canvas, 91 x 162 cm.

Jean Auguste Dominique Ingres,
The Turkish Bath,
Paris, 1862.
Oil on canvas, diameter: 108 cm.

WAS COROT A MODEL?

When Camille Pissarro showed his works at the 1864 Exhibition, he presented himself as a pupil of Corot. When Edgar Degas dreamed of something well done, he cited a "well-ordered whole (Poussin style) and the old age of Corot". When Alfred Sisley spoke about the painters he admired, he mentioned "Delacroix, Corot, Millet, Rousseau, Courbet, our masters". And when Berthe and Edma Morisot decided to work on a motif, outdoors, they turned to Corot, who gave them painting from life lessons next to the lakes of Ville-d'Avray.

These works are located in the **Sully area**, on the **2nd floor**

Camille Corot,
Woman in Blue,
1874.
Oil on canvas, 80 x 50.5 cm.

Camille Corot,
Souvenir of Mortefontaine,
1864.
Oil on canvas, 65 x 89 cm.

HOW DOES ONE GET TO KNOW COLOURS, GILD A PANEL AND GRIND BLACK?

There are seven natural colours in all: yellow ochre, red ochre, green earth, graphite black, slaked lime white, ultramarine blue made of lapis-lazuli, and lead and pewter yellow; in addition to these are man-made colours. Painters only have twenty pigments at their disposal, specified Cennino Cennini, in around 1400, in his *Book of the Art*. For the backgrounds of paintings, wet thoroughly to apply gold leaves. And to grind black, crush it for a long time on porphyry, in clear water, then rub with a spatula.

These works are located in the **Denon wing**, on the 1st floor

Cenni di Pepi, known as **Cimabue**,
The Virgin and Child in majesty surrounded by six angels,
Pisa, circa 1270.
Tempera on wood, 427 x 280 cm.

Giotto di Bondone,
St Francis of Assisi receiving the stigmate,
Pisa, circa 1295-1300.
Tempera on wood, 313 x 163 cm.

Simone Martini,
The carrying of the cross,
Sienna, circa 1335.
Tempera on wood, 28 x 16 cm.

WHY INVENT PERSPECTIVE?

Choose a frame, set a horizon, place a central point where the lines of the picture meet, introduce characters of varying sizes. And tell a story, as if it were the stage of a theatre. These were the rules of geometric perspective as invented in Florence, under the Medicis, at the start of the 15th century, and as applied by Fra Angelico and Uccello. The objective: to establish order, to construct a vision of the world on a human scale. In Florence, at the same time, space was measured by cartography and time by mechanical clocks.

These works are located in the **Denon wing**, on the **1st floor**

Paolo di Dono, known as **Uccello**,
The Battle of San Romano:
the counter-attack by Micheletto da
Cotignola, Florence, circa 1455-1456.
Tempera on wood, 182 x 317 cm.

Guido di Pietro, known as **Fra Angelico**,
The Coronation of the Virgin,
Fiesole, circa 1430-1435.
Tempera on wood, 209 x 206 cm.
Detail of the predella: *The Miracle of the book.*

Through portraits, painting brings back to life the faces of the dead to a certain extent. This is one of its noble missions: so specified the theorist Alberti in his 1434 tract. Because painting contains "a divine force which not only makes absent men present, as friendship is said to do, but moreover makes the dead seem almost alive. Even after many centuries they are recognised with great pleasure and with great admiration for the painter".

❮ "Portrait from Fayoum", p. 41.

These works are located in the **Denon wing,** on the **1ˢᵗ floor**

Domenico di Tommaso Bigordi, known as **Ghirlandaio**, *Portrait of an old man and little boy*, Florence, circa 1488. Tempera on wood, 63 x 46 cm.

_ Above
Antonello da Messina,
Portrait of a man,
known as *Le Condottiere*,
Venice, 1475.
Oil on wood, 36,2 x 30 cm.

_ Top
Piero della Francesca,
Portrait of Sigismondo Malatesta,
Rimini, circa 1451.
Oil on wood, 44 x 34 cm.

_ Above
Antonio di Puccio di Cerreto
or **Antonio Pisano**, known as **Pisanello**,
Portrait of a Princess of Este,
Ferrare, circa 1436-1438.
Oil on wood, 43 x 30 cm.

SHOULD MODERN ARTISTS IMITATE OR SURPASS THE ANCIENTS?

Florence, at the start of the 15th century. Everyone, princes, humanists and artists, considered Antiquity to be the absolute model, an Antiquity discovered or rediscovered through its ruins, its monuments, its statues and its texts. So the edict went out, soon to be widely adopted in Italian courts : let's revive the splendour of the Ancients, let's learn beauty from them, let's integrate their culture to build a better foundation for our own. Botticelli depicted the Graces, ancient goddesses of Beauty or personifications of Love; Mantegna arranged Roman relics and motifs as he pleased.

These works are located in the **Denon wing**, on the **1st floor**

Sandro di Mariano Filipepi, known as **Botticelli**, *Venus and the Graces offering gifts to a young woman*, Florence, circa 1480-1483. Fresco, 211 x 283 cm.

Andrea Mantegna,
St Sebastian,
Mantua, circa 1480.
Tempera on canvas, 255 x 140 cm.

The alert was given on 22 August 1911: *The Mona Lisa* had disappeared! The Louvre was sealed, it was searched from top to bottom, the investigation began. The police arrested several suspects, from an escaped convict to Guillaume Apollinaire who was held for five days at *La Santé*, Paris' central prison. The guilty party was only found two years later: Vincenzo Peruggia, a painter and decorator, had lifted down the painting one day when the museum was closed and calmly taken it home on the bus. He claimed that he had wanted to take it back to its country of origin. Rediscovered in Florence, *Mona Lisa* returned to the museum in 1914, with a smile on her face.

These works are located in the **Denon wing**, on the **1st floor**

Leonardo da Vinci,
The Virgin of the Rocks,
Milan, 1483-1486.
Oil on wood transposed
onto canvas, 199 x 122 cm.

Leonardo da Vinci,
The Virgin and Child with St Anne,
unfinished work,
Milan, circa 1508-1510.
Oil on wood, 168 x 130 cm.

Leonardo da Vinci,
Portrait of Lisa Gherardini del Giocondo,
known as *"La Giaconda"* or *"Mona Lisa"*,
Florence, circa 1503-1506.
Oil on wood, 77 x 53 cm.

⤵ DOES PAINTING AMOUNT TO DECEPTION?

One day, recounts Pliny the Elder, Zeuxis painted grapes that were so true to life that birds came down to peck at them. Rising to this challenge, Parrhasius added a curtain to the painting. Zeuxis asked for the curtain to be pulled aside. Discovering his mistake he conceded defeat. Because whilst *he* had succeeded in fooling the birds, Parrhasius had managed to trick an artist. Famous and celebrated, this legendary story about the two Greek painters forms the basis of one of the principles of the Renaissance: art should imitate nature, the artist must excel at representing its creations. This was the philosophy that Raphael applied in all his works.

These works are located in the **Denon wing,** on the **1st floor**

Raffaello Sanzio, known as **Raphael**,
Portrait of Baldassare Castiglione,
Rome, 1514-1515.
Oil on canvas, 82 x 67 cm.

Raffaello Sanzio, known as **Raphael**,
Virgin and Child with St John the Baptist,
known as *La Belle Jardinière*,
Florence, 1507.
Oil on wood, 122 x 80 cm.

A canvas is delicate and light, it can be tightened on a stretcher, it can be pulled across the walls of palaces and churches, it can be rolled up and is easily transported to a client on the other side of the world. At the end of the 15th century and especially during the 16th century, artists in Venice started using canvases made from linen and hemp for their works: they were easier to handle then heavy wooden panels, they were more resistant to the ravages of time and humidity than frescoes; Titian believed that they were perfect for easel paintings and Veronese thought them ideal for major decorative works.

These works are located in the **Denon wing**, on the **1st floor**

Antonio Allegri, known as **Correggio**, *The Mystic Marriage of St Catherine of Alexandria with St Sebastian*, Parma, circa 1526-1527. Oil on wood, 105 x 102 cm.

Tiziano Vecellio, known as **Titian**, *Man with a Glove*, Venice, circa 1520-1523. Oil on canvas, 100 x 89 cm.

Tiziano Vecellio, known as **Titian**,
The Country Concert,
Venice, circa 1510.
Oil on canvas, 105 x 137 cm.

This work is located in the **Denon wing,** on the **1st floor**

Paolo Caliari, known as **Veronese**,
The Wedding Feast at Cana
(complete work and details),
Venice, 1562-1563.
Oil on canvas, 677 x 994 cm.

WOULD CARAVAGGIO DESTROY PAINTING?

The same name came up time and time again in Roman police reports at the beginning of the 17th century: that of Caravaggio who, irritable, insolent and generally despised, wielding insults and the sword, was sent into exile for murder. Moreover, was he not "born into the world to destroy the art of painting", as Nicolas Poussin accused him of? Conceiving holy and profane pictures in the style of common people, accentuating physical presence, focusing on colour and not drawing, tightening the composition, forcing light contrasts: Caravaggio triggered a veritable revolution, which was to reach the whole of Europe.

These works are located in the **Denon wing**, on the **1ˢᵗ floor**

Michelangelo Merisi, known as **Caravaggio**, *The Death of the Virgin*, painting rejected as being disrespectful by the Carmelites at the Church of Santa Maria della Scala in Trastevere, Rome, 1605-1606. Oil on canvas, 369 x 245 cm.

‹ La Tour and Le Nain, pp. 62-63.

‹ Hals, pp. 110-111.

‹ Rembrandt, pp. 112-113.

Michelangelo Merisi, known as
Caravaggio, *The Fortune-teller*,
Rome, circa 1594.
Oil on canvas, 99 x 131 cm.

In Venice, in the 18th century, Carnival was an ine-vitable subject for painters; focusing in on dancers or masked couples, or panoramic, in an architec-tural décor arranged like a scene from a play, they showed merrymaking, acrobatics and chivalrous games ahead of Lent – during the carnival, people feasted, they ate meat. In Rome, the Naples-born artist Gaspare Traversi depicted other colourful aspects of daily life, with close-up frames of an artist and his model, a brawl or a game of cards.

These works are located in the **Denon wing**, on the **1st floor**

Francesco Guardi,
The Doge of Venice at
Carnival Thursday on the Piazzetta,
Venice, 1766-1770.
Oil on canvas, 67 x 100 cm.

They are innumerable, take on a variety of aspects and form a celestial troop: spiritual in nature, seraphs and cherubs, archangels and angels are the messengers of god who reveal to man his wishes – and when they are fallen, rebellious and tempting, they are working for the devil.

Holding a lily, sometimes an olive branch, the Archangel Gabriel's mission was to tell the Virgin Mary that she would carry the Son of God. Angels of Christianity often had wings, just like the protective spirits and divine forces of ancient civilisations.

❮ *Winged bulls with human heads*, pp. 10-11.
❮ *The Archangel Gabriel reveals Sura VIII (The Spoils) to the Prophet*, p. 27.
❮ *Victory*, p. 49.

These works are located in the **Richelieu wing**, on the **2nd floor**

_ Top
Rogier Van der Weyden,
The Annunciation,
Brussels, circa 1435.
Oil on wood, 86 x 93 cm.

_ Above
Jan Van Eyck,
The Virgin at the home of Chancellor Rolin,
Bruges, circa 1435.
Oil on wood, 66 x 62 cm.

Hans Memling,
Angel holding an Olive Branch,
altarpiece fragment,
Bruges, circa 1480.
Oil on wood, 16.4 x 11 cm.

Whilst Bosch and Bruegel denounced, Metsys pondered. Drifting towards the country of Madness, packed with people, the ship of fools is an allegory of the vices of these men of the 15th century; everyone is corrupt, including people of the Church. Madness turns the world upside down, just as a mirror shows reality in reverse. Whilst it is the instrument of the devil here, it is also the painter's tool and model, which creates and masters the illusion: prominent on the table, a small convex mirror – which condenses by dilating the field of vision – shows the image of an artist who thus ends up placed in the foreground of his work.

Pieter Bruegel, the Elder,
The Beggars,
Brussels, 1568.
Oil on wood, 18 x 21 cm.

Hieronymus Bosch,
The Ship of Fools,
Bois-le-Duc, circa 1490-1500.
Oil on wood, 58 x 32 cm.

Quentin Metsys,
The Moneylender and his wife,
Antwerp, 1514.
Oil on wood, 70 x 67 cm.

DID RUBENS HAVE DELUSIONS OF GRANDEUR?

A highly organised studio where numerous assistants – including Van Dyck – worked for him, a taste for large formats, monumental décors and noble subjects combining contemporary history and allegory, a prestigious commission for twenty-four immense canvases for the palace of the queen mother, a considerable reputation, a colossal fortune, a lot of energy, fullness of movement, a broad technique, giving freshness to flesh and sumptuousness to materials: a great collector of antiquities and a great traveller, Rubens never tired of excess.

These works are located in the **Richelieu wing**, on the **2nd floor**

Antoon Van Dyck,
Charles I at the hunt,
London, circa 1635-1638.
Oil on canvas, 266 x 207 cm.

Peter Paul Rubens,
Helena Fourment with a carriage,
Antwerp, circa 1639.
Oil on wood, 195 x 132 cm.

Peter Paul Rubens,
Peter Paul Rubens,
The Landing at Marseilles
on 3rd November 1600,

9th painting in the series ordered
by Maria de' Medici for a gallery
in the Luxembourg Palace,
Antwerp, 1622-1625.
Oil on canvas, 394 x 295 cm.

In Haarlem, the Dutch town which thrived on its beer and luxury weaving industries, Frans Hals earned a reputation for his large-scale collective portraits as well his character portraits – a prostitute in Bohemian clothes, a jester, musicians and joyful drinkers.

But his prestigious commissions did not prevent him from being permanently short of money and he left a string of debts behind him with traders. Whilst some were eccentric, melancholic or angry, Frans Hals would go down in history as the archetypal extravagant artist.

These works are located in the **Richelieu wing**, on the **2ⁿᵈ floor**

Frans Hals,
The Gypsy Girl,
Haarlem, circa 1628-1630.
Oil on canvas, 58 x 52 cm.

Frans Hals,
The Jester on the Lute,
Haarlem, circa 1624.
Oil on canvas, 70 x 62 cm.

Rembrandt applied his paint thickly, roughly, in relief. On the more illuminated areas, slowly, with a palette knife or with his hands, he worked the texture of the pigments, both to reflect light and create shadow. White lead and chalk were always present.

But it was "so loaded with colour that the painting could have been lifted by grasping the subject's nose", recounted one of his pupils. It was the very thickness of the paint that constituted his trademark: for the best effect, the thickness should be viewed from a distance, advised Rembrandt.

These works are located in the **Richelieu wing**, on the **2nd floor**

**Rembrandt
Harmensz. Van Rijn,**
The Flayed Ox,
Amsterdam, 1655.
Oil on wood, 94 x 69 cm

**Rembrandt
Harmensz. Van Rijn,**
Bathsheba Bathing,
Amsterdam, 1654.
Oil on canvas, 142 x 142 cm.

Rembrandt
Harmensz. Van Rijn,
Portrait of the Artist at his Easel,
Amsterdam, 1660.
Oil on canvas, 111 x 90 cm.

BUT WHO WAS VERMEER?

During his era, the Master of Delft was certainly not one of those artists that go unrecognised; people travelled a long way to see him, such was his reputation. In his studio, he often had nothing to sell, his works having been placed with merchants. Moreover, he did not paint to make a living and he produced barely four works per year. He did not invent any of his themes, interiors that were typical of Dutch art – like Pieter de Hooch.

What he did invent was their intimacy, their light, their conception, their figures that were both near and distant. Vermeer died at the age of forty-three, leaving behind barely forty canvases.

Pieter de Hooch,
Young Woman Drinking,
Delft, 1658.
Oil on canvas, 69 x 60 cm.

Johannes Vermeer,
The Astronomer,
Delft, 1668.
Oil on canvas, 51 x 45 cm.

Johannes Vermeer,
The Lacemaker,
Delft, circa 1670-1671.
Oil on canvas mounted on wood,
24 x 21 cm.

MAN OR WOMAN, WHAT ARE THE RIGHT MEASUREMENTS?

It is well known that female anatomy has no perfect measurement – so Raphael emphasised when he wrote to Baldassare Castiglione: "Beauty is so rare in a woman that I use an idea produced by my imagination". Because, as the Bible says, Eve was not created by God originally but came from the rib of man. These were not the principles followed by Dürer when, in his *Four Books on Human Proportions*, he recorded all body types, female and male, from "the villager, fat and stout" to the most fragile. Everything in nature is worthy of study.

❮ Raphael, pp. 94-95.

These works are located in the **Richelieu wing**, on the **2nd floor**

Hans Holbein, the Younger,
Nikolas Kratzer,
London, 1528.
Oil on wood, 83 x 67 cm.

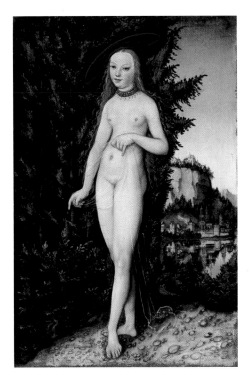

Lucas Cranach, the Elder,
Venus standing in a Landscape,
Wittenberg, 1529.
Oil on wood, 33 x 26 cm.

Albrecht Dürer,
Portrait of the Artist holding a Thistle,
Nuremberg, 1493.
Oil on parchment mounted on canvas,
56.5 x 44.5 cm.

WHAT DID FRIEDRICH SEE?

At the beginning of the 19th century, in the era of German Romanticism, melancholy was embodied in what was known as the "evil of the world", a rejection of the real and realism. With or without a figure, Friedrich's landscapes reveal a threatening universe, as well as solitude, tension, a resonance of the divine and death. "An artist should portray not only what is before his eyes but what he sees in himself. But if he sees nothing in himself, he would do well not to paint what he sees before his eyes either." A radical piece of advice.

These works are located in the **Richelieu wing**, on the **2nd floor**

Caspar David Friedrich,
The Tree of Crows,
Germany, circa 1822.
Oil on canvas, 59 x 74 cm.

Caspar David Friedrich,
The Moon Rising over the Sea,
circa 1818.
Oil on canvas, 22 × 30 cm.

"The Chinese, who are so interested in the paintings of their own country, have little taste for European works, in which, they say, there are too many black patches. That is how they describe shadows", reported Du Bos in 1719. Only an outside view of western vision could highlight what otherwise seems natural. It was only from the 15th century that cast shadows began to play a central role, positioning figures in space, giving the illusion of depth, accentuating contours, dramatising representations – a crucified body or a beggar on the ground.

These works are located in the **Denon wing**, on the **1st floor**

Domenikos Theotokopoulos,
known as **El Greco**,
Christ on the Cross adored by two donors,
Toledo, 1576-1579.
Oil on canvas, 260 x 171 cm.

Francisco de Zurbarán,
St Apollonia,
Seville, circa 1636.
Oil on canvas, 116 x 66 cm.

Bartolomé Esteban Murillo,
The Young Beggar,
Seville, circa 1650.
Oil on canvas, 134 x 110 cm.

Goya did everything: tapestry cartoons for the palaces of Madrid, religious works, decoration of cupolas, portraits of the nobility, pastoral landscapes, effigies of the royal family, beautiful images of the Marquesa de La Solana and the Duchess of Alba, bull races, a thousand drawings, the *Caprices* and *Disasters of War etchings*, a gun fight, a few still-life works including a sheep's head, several self-portraits, fourteen black paintings in his "House of the Deaf", miniatures on ivory and a milkwoman from Bordeaux.

These works are located in the **Denon wing**, on the **1ˢᵗ floor**

Francisco de Goya y Lucientes,
Woman with Fan,
Madrid, 1805-1810.
Oil on canvas, 103 x 83 cm.

Francisco de Goya y Lucientes,
Portrait of the Condesa del Carpio,
known as *The Marquesa de la Solana*,
Madrid, circa 1793-1794.
Oil on canvas, 181 x 122 cm.

LANDSCAPE OR PORTRAIT, WHICH OF THE TWO STYLES PREVAILED?

He brought back branches, moss, fragments of glass and rock to his studio and from these little pieces of nature he composed imaginary landscapes for his own pleasure only. Because wealthy customers only wanted large portraits: Although Gainsborough com-plied with their wishes, he placed the majority of his models on a green and bucolic background. Following his death, but only after his death, Reynolds, his long-standing rival, who had official commissions and earned twice as much, and who placed historical paintings above all else, paid homage to him at the Royal Academy.

These works are located in the **Sully area**, on the **1ˢᵗ floor**

Thomas Gainsborough,
Conversation in a park,
London, circa 1746-1747.
Oil on canvas, 73 x 68 cm.

Joshua Reynolds,
Master Hare,
London, circa 1788-1789.
Oil on canvas, 77 x 63 cm.

IS IT REALLY FINISHED?

Between the polished and the sketched, the smooth and the rough, the complete and the incomplete, the finished article and the *non finito*, in short the finished and the unfinished, arguments have raged since the Renaissance; three centuries later, it still raged amongst landscape artists. A collector called James Lenox took receipt in New York of a canvas by Turner that he had just bought. Enquiring about his reaction, the painter asked: "So, what does he think of the painting?". "He finds it to be undefined", came the reply. To which Turner retorted: "Tell him that the indefinable is my forte".

These works are located in the **Sully area**, on the **1st floor**

John Constable,
*Weymouth Bay
with approaching storm*,
England, circa 1819.
Oil on canvas, 88 x 112 cm.

Joseph Mallord William Turner,
*Landscape with a River and a Bay
in the Distance*,
England, circa 1835-1840.
Oil on canvas, 93 x 123 cm.

le pied de côté dans l'étrier
quelquefois

le drapeau dans son étui effilé
devant la tente

la plaine et la tribu rouge quelquefois
vers le fond. — devant demi douzaine
de cavaliers dans la fumée. un homme
plus en avant, burnous bleu. très foncé

— en avant nous tournant le dos la
ligne de soldats précédés du Caïd et
des drapeaux.

la course des cinq ou six cavaliers.

le jeune homme tête nue, Caftan vert
vissang:
le nègre bonnet pointu. Caftan bleu.

les hommes éclairés sur le bord de côté. l'ombre des
objets blancs très reflétée en bleu. le rouge des selles et du
turban presque noir.

au passage du gué les hommes grouillant. un cheval
blanc

GRAPHIC ARTS

Eugène Delacroix,
pages from a notebook
depicting travels in Morocco, 1832.
Watercolour and graphite
on paper,
one page: 16.5 x 9.8 cm.

When used to lay the groundwork for a painting, drawing takes the form of a rough sketch, a study, a model or a cartoon. Whether it is for perspective, composition or execution, whether it is done in the classical style or from life, in a museum or outside, it establishes the broad lines and locates the figures, defines the drape of a curtain and the shape of a branch and even shows how light should fall. Autonomous, an aide-mémoire or exploration, it scrutinises the folds in a landscape and the expression of a face.

Leonardo da Vinci,
Drapery for a Kneeling Figure,
Italy, late 15th to early 16th century.
Grey tempera with white highlights
on grey canvas, 20.7 x 28.1 cm.

Jean Fouquet,
Caesar crossing the Rubicon,
page extracted from *Ancient History
as far as Caesar and the Deeds of the
Romans,* Tours, circa 1470-1475.
Illumination on vellum, 44 x 32.5 cm.

Antonio di Puccio di Cerreto or
Antonio Pisano, known as **Pisanello**,
Great Spotted Woodpecker and *Tufted
Lapwing*, Italy, 15th Century.
Watercolour with white highlights,
brown ink and black chalk on vellum,
9 x 14.7 cm and 15.7 x 28.9 cm.

Albrecht Dürer,
The Arco Valley,
Italy, 1495.
Watercolour and gouache with black
ink highlights on parchment,
22.3 x 22.2 cm.

Peter Paul Rubens,
Study of trees,
Antwerp, 17th century.
Black chalk and brown ink on paper,
58.2 x 48.9 cm.

Rembrandt Harmensz.
Van Rijn,
Oriental head with a Bird of Paradise,
Amsterdam, circa 1638.
Brown ink and white gouache
highlights on paper, 17.8 x 16.9 cm.

Charles Le Brun,
*Three men's heads in relation
to a screech owl*,
Paris, circa 1668.
Black ink gouache and black chalk
on white paper, 23.1 x 32 cm.

It is applied using hatching, in blurred or well-blended touches. Several layers of colours can be placed on top of each other; there is no need to rub out to re-do and continue the drawing. The artist works quickly, which means models do not have to spend hours posing; on a sheet of paper, just the face is drawn. Later, in the studio, the artist joins it up to the whole, sticking together all the sheets on a large canvas. And the crayon matter is used to give the skin its various nuances: pastels are ideal for producing portraits.

Maurice Quentin Delatour,
known as **Quentin de La Tour**,
Portrait of the Marquise de Pompadour,
Paris, 1755. Pastel with gouache
highlights on grey-blue paper mounted
on canvas, 177.5 x 130 cm.

Jean-Baptiste Siméon Chardin,
Self-portrait with spectacles,
Paris, 1771.
Pastel on grey-blue paper,
45.9 x 37.5 cm.

SCULPTURES

In the foreground: *Apollo* by Nicolas Coustou and *Daphné* by Guillaume Coustou, the Elder, 1714.
In the background: *Mercury astride Pegasus* and *Fame* by Antoine Coysevox, 1699-1701.

Romanesque churches are devoted to images. Becoming its own décor, the architecture entrusts the doorways, the stained-glass windows and even the keystones with recounting holy history, if necessary forcing characters to fit within an imposed framework. No wall remains bare, no column unsculpted. And whilst enthroned Virgins sometimes act as reliquaries and come out during pilgrimages, polychrome groups depict edifying scenes from the Old and New Testaments. Romanesque churches are a bible for the illiterate.

These works are located in the **Denon wing**, on the **ground floor**

Virgin and Child.
Auvergne, second half of the
12th century. Walnut with traces
of polychromy,
h: 84 cm.

Daniel in the lions' pit.
Paris, early 12th century.
Marble, 49 x 53 x 51 cm.

Christ on the Descent from the Cross.
Burgundy, circa 1150.
Wood with traces of gilding
and polychromy, h: 155 cm.

To mark the power of a great figure, there is nothing more striking than a sculpture in the round, which creates its own space and holds its own against the real and human presence: when one is Lord of La Roche-Pot, seneschal of the Duke of Burgundy and chamberlain to Louis XI, it is possible to depict, as if it were taking place in front of us, a great funeral procession with a recumbent statue carried by eight weeping figures, the whole assembly painted and gilded. As for bas-relief, a work that can be seen from one side only, it makes use of the contrasts between the smooth and the creased, light and shade.

These works are located in the **Richelieu wing**, on the **ground floor**

Tomb of Philippe Pot.
Cîteaux, abbey-church, circa 1475.
Painted stone, h: 182 cm.

_ Top
King Childebert.
Paris, Abbey of St-Germain-des-Prés,
1239-1244.
Stone with traces of polychromy,
h: 191 cm.

_ Above
Jean Goujon,
Nymph and spirit,
Paris, Fontaine des Innocents,
circa 1547-1549.
Stone, 73 x 195 cm.

sculptures 141

In order to portray an era of conflict and effort, sculptors oppose diagonals in space, create twists and convulsions, superimpose zigzagging planes and throw forces off balance. Battling with a horse that needs to be broken and an enraged lion, or poised to rush forward, their characters are deliberately chosen: because he wanted to split a tree trunk with his hands, the athlete Milon of Crotona remained immobilised and was attacked by wild animals; sporting winged sandals, Mercury is the messenger of the gods, aiding passage, movement, exchange.

‹ Sculptures from Marly park, pp. 136-137.

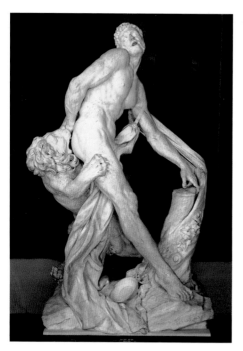

These works are located in the **Marly courtyard** on the **ground floor**

Pierre Puget,
Milon of Crotona,
Versailles, Château gardens, 1682.
Marble, h: 270 cm.

Jean-Baptiste Pigalle,
Mercury Fastening his Winged Sandals,
1744.
Marble, h: 59 cm.

Guillaume Coustou, the Elder,
Loose horse being restrained by a groom,
Marly, château gardens, 1739-1745.
The two *Horses of Marly* were placed
at the entry to the avenue
des Champs-Élysées in 1795.
Marble, h: 355 cm

DOES THE BODY PROVIDE A LESSON IN ANATOMY, ART OR EROTICISM?

When he arrived on the throne, Charles X took what he deemed to be an urgent measure, ordering that the nudity of some of the statues at the Louvre be concealed using vine leaves. This was partly implemented. Because there was danger, there was an offence to decency, parents scarcely dared take their children into the rooms of the museum, wrote the director of the Fine Arts museum in 1824, Viscount Sosthène de La Rochefoucauld, who continued: "Young ladies who cultivate art must refrain from contemplating and studying the most beautiful models if they have not lost all sense of modesty."

Gregor Erhart,
Mary Magdalene,
Augsburg, early 16th century.
Painted lime, h: 177 cm.

Michelangelo Buonarroti,
known as **Michel-Ange,**
Slave, known as *"The Dying Slave",*
unfinished sculpture,
Rome, 1513-1515.
Marble, h: 228 cm.

Antonio Canova,
Psyché revived by Cupid's Kiss,
Rome, 1793.
Marble, h: 155 cm.

OBJETS D'ART

The Great Drawing Room of the Duc de Morny, minister of Napoleon III, 1856-1861.

WHAT DO TREASURES HOLD?

In churches and cathedrals, hidden from the view of everyone, displayed on the altar or brought out for pilgrimages, can be found objects of worship and the insignia of royalty – reliquaries, ciboria, monstrances and sceptres. Objects which are precious because of what they are made of but also because of the relics they may hide; thus, from the life of Christ are preserved, within treasures scattered across Europe, the Shroud of Turin, the Holy Prepuce, the Crown of Thorns, the fragment of the True Cross, the nails of the Passion, the Holy Lance, the Precious Blood and the Holy Grail.

These works are located in the **Richelieu wing**, on the **1st floor**

Liturgical Ewer, known as the "Suger Eagle". Vase from Egypt or Rome, mounting produced before 1147. Treasury of the Abbey of St-Denis. Red porphyry, gilded, engraved, chiselled and nielloed silver, h: 43.1 cm.

Equestrian statuette of Charlemagne or Charles the Bald. Metz, cathedral treasury, 9th century. Bronze with traces of gilding, h: 23.5 cm.

The Emperor Triumphant,
known as the "Barberini ivory",
Constantinople,
first half of the 6th century.
Ivory, 34.2 x 26.8 cm.

These works are located in the **Richelieu wing**, on the **1ˢᵗ floor**

Virgin with Child.
Paris, Sainte-Chapelle treasury,
circa 1260-1270.
Ivory with traces of gilding
and polychromy, h: 41 cm.

Descent from the Cross.
Paris, circa 1260-1280.
Ivory with traces of gilding
and polychromy.

Sceptre of Charles V (detail).
Paris, treasury of the Abbey of St-Denis,
1364-1380.
Gold formerly enamelled, gilded silver,
pearls, rubies and coloured glass,
h: 60 cm.

Reliquary-statuette (detail),
known as *Virgin with Child*
by Jeanne d'Évreux.
Paris, treasury of the Abbey of St-Denis,
1324-1339.

Gilded silver, translucent enamels
on basse-taille, gold, rock crystal,
pearls and precious stones,
h: 69 cm.

Ceramics give rise to portraits, architectural décors as well as an astonishing dish on which a larger than life gladiator is roaming about, moulded in relief, from life: the author was an artist in glass, a surveyor, an enamellist, potter and caver, who sometimes gave nature lessons about rivers and springs, metals, salts, stones, clays and enamels, promising four crowns to whoever could get the better of him! "I prefer to tell the truth in my own rustic language, than to lie using rhetoric", announced Bernard Palissy.

These works are located in the **Richelieu wing**, on the 1ˢᵗ **floor**

Bernard Palissy,
Dish decorated with "rustic figulines",
France, circa 1560.
Glazed terracotta, 52.5 x 40.2 cm.

Léonard Limosin,
Portrait of the High Constable
Anne de Montmorency,
Limoges, 1556.
Painted enamel on copper,
gilded wood mounting, 72 x 56 cm.

Masséot Abaquesne,
*Altar step of the chapel of the
château of La Bâtie d'Urfé,*
Rouen, 1557.
Faience, 326 x 184 cm.

HOW IS A WARDROBE OR A CROWN MADE?

It was a veritable army of artisans that, in the royal factories of the 18th century, was responsible for furnishing important residences. The production of an item of furniture involved the cabinetmaker, the wood turner, the ornamentalist, the inlayer, the gilder, the silverer, the carver, the bronze artist, the marble worker, the horn worker, the tortoiseshell inlayer, the mother-of-pearl inlayer, the ivory sculptor, the varnisher, the chair carpenter, the upholsterer... And to create a coronation crown required a silversmith, a gold beater, a jeweller, a lapidary, a diamond cutter, a setter, a polisher, an embroiderer, a velvet weaver...

These works are located in the **Richelieu wing,** on the 1st **floor**

● _ Top, left

Augustin Duflot, according to the drawings of Claude Rondé, *Coronation crown of Louis XV*, Paris, 1722. Gilded silver, plate reproductions of previous stones and embroidered satin, h: 24 cm.

● _ Top, right

The Régent.
Diamond discovered in India in 1698, cut in England at the start of the 18th century and acquired by the Regent in 1717. 140.64 metric carats.

_ Opposite

Charles Cressent,
Monkey Commode, Paris,
circa 1735-1740. Made from fir and
oak, satinwood and amaranth veneer,
gilded bronze and marble, h: 90 cm.

André Charles Boulle,
Wardrobe, Paris, circa 1700.
Made from oak, ebony and amaranth
veneer, marquetry of brass, tin, horn,
tortoiseshell, and coloured wood,
gilded bronze, h: 260 cm.

AFRICAN, ASIAN, OCEANIAN AND AMERICAN ARTS

"Pavillon des Sessions" room.
In the foreground, on the left:
royal mask from Cameroon,
19th century.

WHAT IS A SCULPTOR'S GAZE?

A sculpture is real when it has a look, wrote Giacometti with respect to the works of du Vanuatu: "It is not a representation of an eye, it is well and truly a gaze. Everything else supports the gaze. On the other hand, Greek sculpture has no gaze. It is the body that I look at and analyse. Then something strange happens. In Egyptian sculpture, which has always greatly troubled and appealed to me, there is the Scribe, whose eyes were produced with glass or stones. The eye itself has been represented as closely as possible. But the Scribe doesn't gaze at you." The trick is to impart a gaze without imitating the eye. Because only the gaze counts.

❮ Crouching Scribe, p. 33.

❮ Greek Sculpture, pp. 46-49.

These works are located in the **Marly courtyard, Porte des Lions**

_ Top, left
Male head.
South-West Nigeria, Yoruba region,
Ife culture,
12th-14th century.
Terracotta, h: 15.5 cm.

_ Below, left
Swan and white whale mask.
Alaska, Kuskokwim river region,
Napaskiak village, Yup'ik (Inuit) culture,
early 20th century.
Painted wood and feathers, h: 72 cm.

_Opposite *Müyü ne bu*:
magic stone used for buying
castrated male pigs. Vanuatu,
North of Ambryn Island,
18th-early 19th century.
Volcanic tuff, h: 35.5 cm.

Adu zatua: ancestral statue.
Indonesia, North of Nias Island,
19th century.
Wood with red patina,
h: 55.7 cm.

Female figure.
Mexico, Chupicuaro,
600-100 BC.
Slipped terracotta,
h: 31 cm.

CREDITS

Artlys/De Kerland A.: p. 4; Musée du Quai-Branly/Boy de la Tour Didier : p. 156-157 ; Musée du Quai-Branly/Dubois Hughes : p. 158, 159; RMN/Arnaudet D.: p. 3, 14, 60, 73, 77, 80, 90, 107, 117, 118, 148, 150, 152, 154, 158; RMN/Arnaudet D./Blot G.: p. 63; RMN/Blot G./Christian J.: p. 67; RMN/Arnaudet D./Schormans J.: p. 48; RMN/Beck-Coppola M.: p. 140, 150, 151, 154; RMN/Berizzi J.-G.: p. 56, 58, 70, 73, 84, 86, 89, 91, 94, 95, 119, 130, 131, 132, 148, 158 ; RMN/Bernard P.: p. 13, 65; RMN/Blot G. : p. 41, 57, 63, 70, 76, 81, 84, 85, 101, 103, 104, 105, 110, 112, 114, 120, 122, 128-129, 133, 134, 142, 151 ; RMN/Blot G./Schormans J.: p. 92; RMN/Chuzeville: p. 16, 18, 23, 30, 31, 32, 35, 36, 39, 52, 149, 154, 155; RMN/Hatala B.: p. 102; RMN/Jean C.: p. 89, 104, 106, 108, 120, 121, 138, 141, 142, 145, 153; RMN/Jean C./Schormans J.: p. 53 ; RMN/Lagiewski: p. 17; RMN/Larrieu Ch.: p. 36; RMN/Le Mage T.: p. 79, 96, 103 ; RMN/Leroy P.: p. 52; RMN/Lewandowski H.: couverture, p. 12, 15, 18, 19, 20-21, 22, 24, 25, 27, 28-29, 30, 32, 34, 38, 40, 42-43, 44, 45, 46, 47, 48, 50, 51, 52, 60, 68, 69, 71, 75, 78, 79, 80, 82, 87, 88, 93, 108, 113, 116, 125, 126, 135, 138 ; RMN/Mathéus: p.152 ; RMN/Ojeda R. G.: p. 59, 61, 72, 74, 83, 89, 100, 106, 114, 115, 123, 131, 139, 143, 144 ; RMN/Ojeda R. G./Néri P.: p. 96; RMN/Ollivier T.: p. 24 ; RMN/Raux F.: p. 33, 62, 66, 67; RMN: p. 10-11, 16, 17, 18, 26, 34, 37, 49, 54-55, 64, 92, 97, 98, 99, 109, 124, 127, 130, 133, 142; RMN/Rose C.: p. 6, 136-137, 146-147; RMN/Schormans J.: p. 111, 112, 117.

Artlys Director of Publication: Denis Kilian
Editorial and iconographic coordination: Karine Barou
Graphic design and production:
atelier Juliane Cordes, assisted by Corinne Dury
Computer-aided publishing: Hervé Delemotte
Production: Pierre Kegels
Plans: Thierry Lebreton and Dominique Bissière

© musée du Louvre, Paris, 2006
ISBN: 978-2-35031-102-9

© Artlys, Versailles, 2006
ISBN: 978-2-85495-274-2

Achevé d'imprimer en mai 2012
par Imprimerie Comelli
Dépôt légal : juin 2012